DENMARK

WORLD ADVENTURES

BY STEFFI CAVELL-CLARKE

BookLife

BookLife
PUBLISHING

©2018
BookLife Publishing
King's Lynn
Norfolk PE30 4LS

A catalogue record for this book is available from the British Library.

ISBN: 978-1-78637-394-6

Written by:
Steffi Cavell-Clarke

Edited by:
Kirsty Holmes

Designed by:
Jasmine Pointer

DENMARK
WORLD ADVENTURES

CONTENTS

Words in **bold** can be found in the glossary on page 24.

WHERE IS DENMARK?

Denmark is a small country found in the western part of Europe. It includes hundreds of small

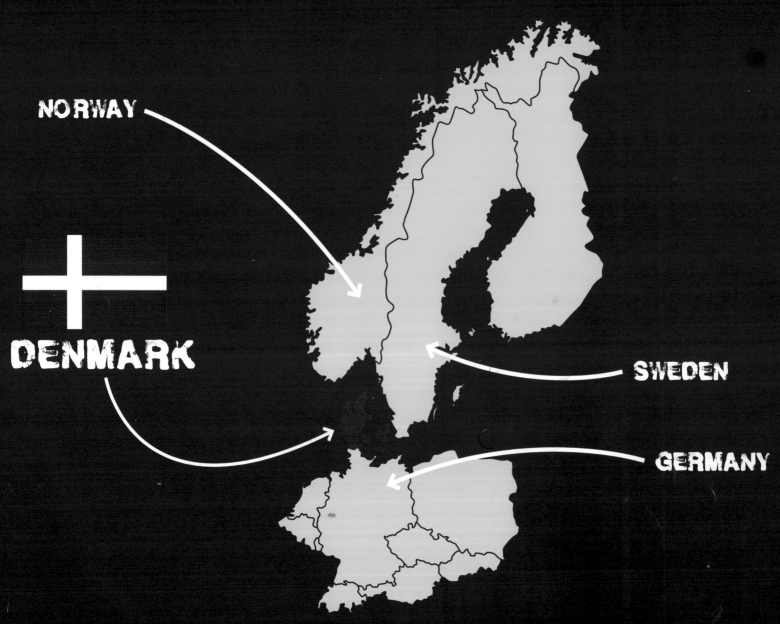

NORWAY

DENMARK

SWEDEN

GERMANY

COPENHAGEN

The capital city of Denmark is Copenhagen, which is on the island of Zealand.

The **population** of Denmark is over 5.7 million. Many people live in the capital city.

WEATHER AND LANDSCAPE

The weather in Denmark is often very windy and wet, but it does change with the seasons. It is usually milder in the summer and colder in the winter.

Denmark has a very flat landscape without any mountains. There are over 400 named islands, which have long **coastlines** and sandy beaches.

The largest island in Denmark is Zealand.

CLOTHING

Most people in Denmark wear **modern** and comfortable clothing, such as jeans and t-shirts.

T-SHIRT

JEANS

At some **festivals**, people might wear **traditional** clothing. Some Danish women will wear long dresses and bonnets.

BONNET

RELIGION

The religion with the most followers in Denmark is Christianity. The Christian place of **worship** is a church. Many Christians visit a church every Sunday for prayer.

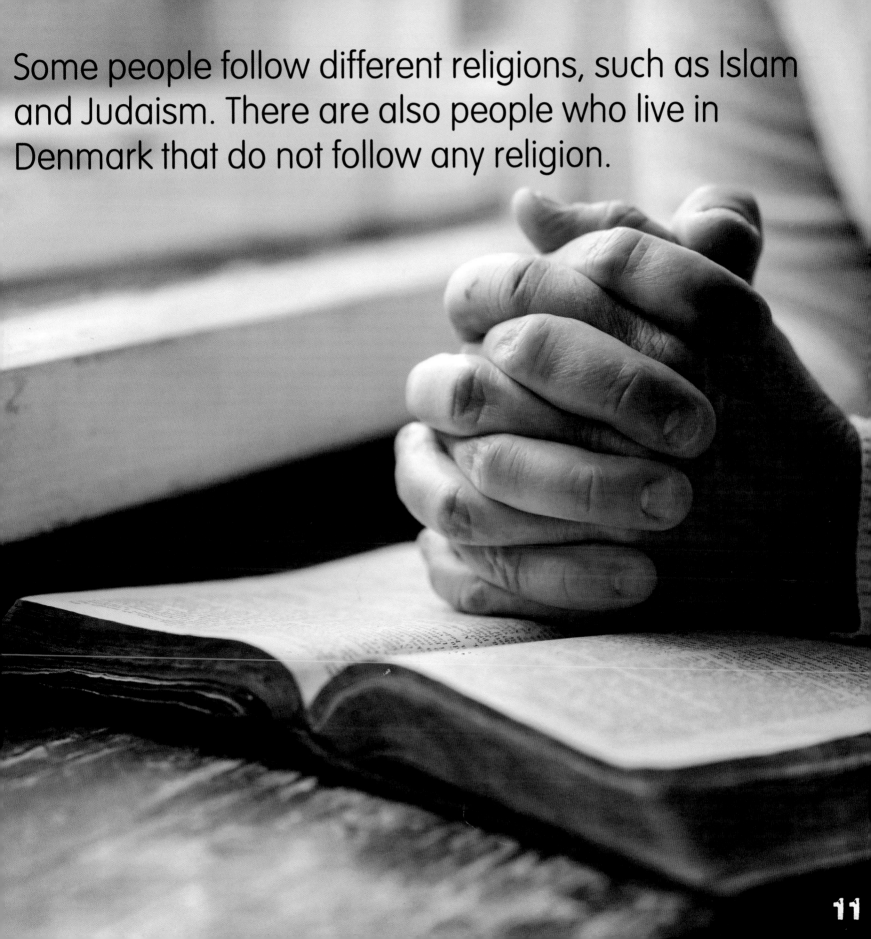

Some people follow different religions, such as Islam and Judaism. There are also people who live in Denmark that do not follow any religion.

FOOD

DANISH PASTRY

The Danish pastry is a sweet pastry. Danish pastries come in many different shapes and have different toppings, such as chocolate and icing.

Rye bread is a traditional Danish bread. It is used when making open sandwiches and is eaten mostly for lunch with a topping, such as cold meats or eggs.

OPEN SANDWICH

AT SCHOOL

At school, children learn how to read and write.
They also study subjects such as science, geography
and history.

Children also learn how to play sport at school, such as athletics and football.

Many children also learn how to swim at school.

AT HOME

APARTMENTS

Most people who live in Denmark live in **urban** areas, such as towns and cities. There are many different types of homes to live in, such as houses or apartments.

Many people live in small villages and towns along the coastlines. There are also people that live and work on farms.

FAMILIES

Many children in Denmark live with their parents and their **siblings** at home. They can also live with other family members, such as their grandparents.

Danish families like to get together to celebrate specials occasions such as weddings and birthdays. They often celebrate by eating special food and singing songs.

SPORT

Football is one of the most popular sports in Denmark. Many people go to watch their favourite football team play.

There are many other popular sports, such as cycling, swimming, ice hockey and basketball.

FUN FACTS

Danish people have a special word, which is "hygge". Hygge means **cosy** and peaceful.

Hygge is pronounced Hoo-ke.

Hans Christian Andersen was a famous Danish author and poet. He wrote many fairy tales, such as The Snow Queen, The Little Mermaid and The Ugly Duckling.

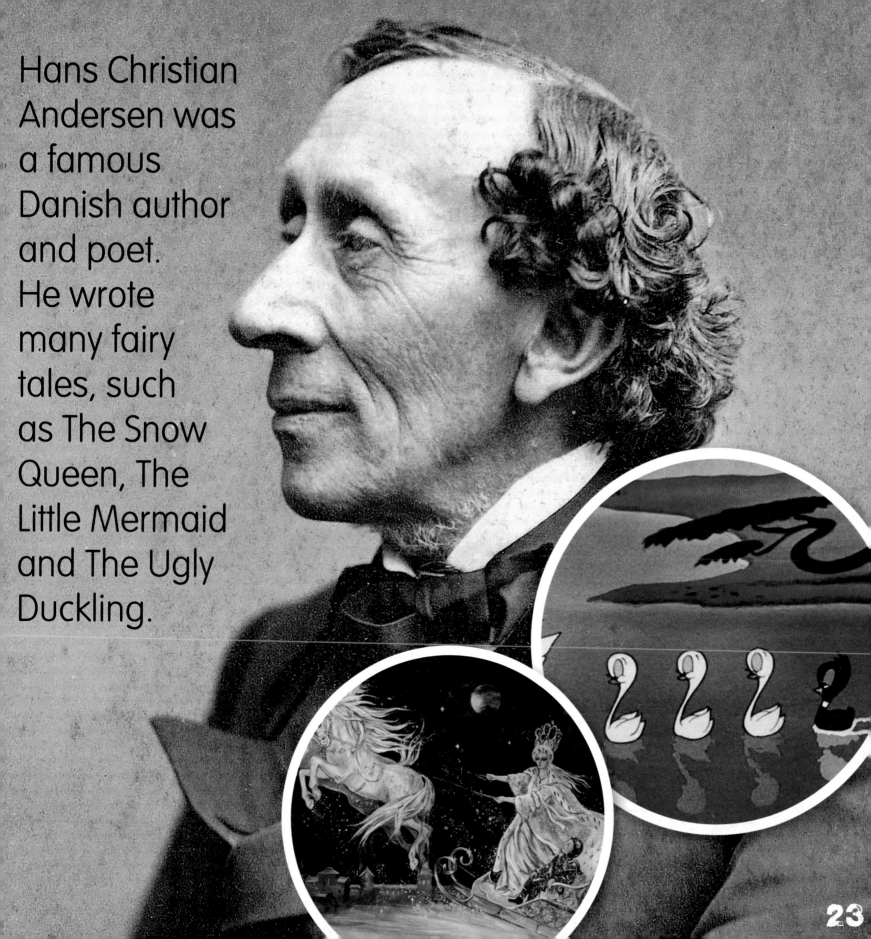

GLOSSARY

coastlines	areas of land that meet the sea
cosy	a feeling of comfort and warmth
festivals	special occasions that are celebrated
islands	areas of land surrounded by water
modern	something from present or recent times
population	number of people living in a place
siblings	brothers and sisters
traditional	ways of behaving that have been done for a long time
urban	a town or city
worship	a religious act such as praying

INDEX

Photocredits: Abbreviations: l-left, r-right, b-bottom, t-top, c-centre, m-middle.
All images are courtesy of Shutterstock.com, unless stated otherwise.

Front Cover, 24 – Aleksey Klints. 2 – LaMiaFotografia. 3 – raysay. 4 – boreala. 5 – S-F. 6 – Savvapanf Photo. 7t – t. 7b – Dennis Jacobsen. 8bl – William Perugini. 8tr – Be Good. 9 – KN. 10 – Nakcrub. 11 – Halfpoint. 12 – UNIKYLUCKK. 13 – VVDVVD. 14 – ESB Professional. 15t – SpeedKingz. 15b – Africa Studio. 16 – Allard One. 17 – Wila_Photo. 18 – Monkey Business Images. 19 – jean schweitzer. 20 – JTKPHOTO. 20r – Iurii Osadchi. 21l – Marivdav. 21rt – Alla Iatsun. 21rm – Grandpa. 21rb – MaszaS. 22 – Milosz Maslanka. 23m – By Thora Hallager (1821-1884) – http://museum.odense.dk/viden-om/hc-andersen/publikationer/jeg-sad-i-dag-for-photographen.aspx, Public Domain, https://commons.wikimedia.org/w/index.php?curid=11819411. 23br – By OswaldLR – BD, Public Domain, https://commons.wikimedia.org/w/index.php?curid=42118155. 23bl – By Elena Ringo http://www.elena-ringo.com, CC BY 3.0, https://commons.wikimedia.org/w/index.php?curid=37744268.